Leadership Perspective: Ideation of Ecosystems for Digital Transformation

By

Dr. Amanyi Vincent

Table of Contents

Acknowledgments

I am very grateful to God and to my family for the great support all through the way to this point of my journey in life. I dedicate this book to my dad, who left the scene about twenty years ago, who made sure, with the effort of my mum, that I have a basic first-degree education from the university.

Abstract

Digital technology is a driver that could optimize the enterprise business-technology landscape in a transparent manner through robust business process orientation if implemented well. The purpose of this book is to provide a comprehensive analysis of the evolution of the digital ecosystem in organizations regardless of size. The book framework consisted of multiple layered value creation concepts in enterprise across business domains, starting from early adoption to mature technology environment.

In addition, the book was able to lay out core capabilities that would enable your digital landscape to achieve a mature enterprise information system with robust security features that would be visible to end users. The book also listed that, in addition to improving the performance within multiple interfaces of partners/actors, true technology helps enable cost savings that are critical to achieving financial benefits in business enterprises apart from monetizing your ecosystem. Harmonizing your technological landscape is very vital to better orchestrate and establish the best-in-class total cost of ownership while creating flexible and modular solutions for the future.

Chapter One

Introduction

Business process orientation is one of the oldest aspects of change framework in enabling technological change in organizations to become viable within the market space. If a corporation wants to become successful in competitive markets, both its business fundamentals and technology should fit together to have aligned goals to enable desired results. The concept of technology integration does not exist as an absolute business unit within an organization without input from the business domain of the organization, and the flow of information among stakeholders is critical to establish a competitive advantage at an enterprise level. Structured technology drives the flow of information among all respective business stakeholders, and the innovative nature of the technology will go a long way to create value for organizational ecosystems. Multiple technologies have been widely published by industry players to have the advantage of enabling performance and optimization.

The migration to a digital platform by various business applications has resulted in innovation within the business community to drive the much-needed change within the organization. No organization can exist without the concept of managing enterprise information from multiple node points to support everyday operational needs. Data itself is useless without a clear definition, and mapping data from multiple sources require understanding your business needs with organizational targeted vision will go a long way to enable the growth direction. The scope of this book is to provide anyone in an organization with a comprehensive perception of understanding the fundamentals of data structure and how it could be replicated in any business enterprise by customizing the process as "fit" to generate tangible value overall.

There is a great need to review your current business landscape, and some hard questions need to be asked to give you a better understanding if your business is ready for digital transformation or if your current landscape is ready to begin the digital journey. A comprehensive assessment of your enterprise will provide a 360 overview of where some level of a project needs to be plugged in to enable the fundamentals of digital capability. Some indicators from the assessment should detail the current state of data structure and capture the true state of an event in the organization. Every organization, regardless of its size, needs. The journey from the last century to date comes with some steep learning and understanding our life has drastically changed, the paradigm is a 360 shift based on different milestones, which has seen lots of mergers and acquisitions across different business verticals.

The one common driver in this whole journey is Data even though we have walked through various transformations, modernization of our business landscape has shaped the maturity of different industries and our whole civilization. The traditional business rules never emphasized the continuous growth of data due to the lack of understanding of how to clearly tie business strategy to technology. But then, today's technology has proved otherwise from all fronts, thanks to the emergence of the different platform's across the world, which overall has pushed the value of data as a steroid for forward-thinking organizations.

There is a need to review your data and understand the type of value you are currently seeing from an enterprise lens to gain better visibility across all node points within the organization. The fact has always rested on data structure and organizational process maturity to plan for the future with a great competitive advantage. It all starts with reviewing your current business process to see if it fits in with the elastic growth pathway, both in vertical and horizontal directions within the market space. The meta-data fundamental is very critical here, which could be restructured or designed to predict intelligent information to multi-layered stakeholders. Some of the questions that should come to mind are what is the best way to structure my data to quickly respond to both everyday operational needs and strategic partners? The best approach to answering this question is to set up a steering committee to do a deep dive and unravel a good use case that will stand the test of time.

As business owners, investors, and organization leaders should always have a 360-degree culture check to provide a better perspective on how the organization will perform in both the short term and long term. Culture is a living thing in the modern organization, which makes it impossible to avoid the subject, as the concept of traditional organizational behavior has died on the middle floor of the organization even though it is still currently being taught in most research institutions across the world. Cultural rhythm stimulates hard-to-talk in an organization for change at the top and bottom of the organization. Business across various verticals is currently witnessing unprecedented innovation pressure to remain competitive, due to rapid technological change and industry disruption acceleration. The increased point of digital use cases has enabled a predicted technology landscape where networks are linking individuals, organizations, and nations as never before. The growth of ideation among the business community does stimulate the conversation to exchange ideas and cross-fertilize innovative impulses across organizational boundaries. The start of experimentation of ideas is a good place to start but requires discipline enforcement at every node point of the organization processes, both at a strategic and tactical level.

The art and science culture change in an organization comes with doing something differently beyond the normal execution plans to adopting a mechanism of busting hierarchy that often sap out creativity. Some of this hierarchy comes with embedded constraints that limit innovation capabilities in different ways and forms.

The world is made of ordinary people with extraordinary minds, harnessing the best of these minds requires a candid conversation that would drive unconventional thinking. These cultures embrace diverse thinking that believes every idea is good, and any bad idea is only yet to be exploited, which would require building a good case to justify the ideation. When leaders utilize the approach of "think outside the box," it means they are creating an innovative atmosphere, which could sometimes start with a brief conversation and brainstorming session at a regular interval. The leader is, in most cases, encouraging the unreasonable, which will end up with improved change culture, as practiced by most fortune 500 technology leadership.

As the saying goes, "Customer is the king".The creation of any product or service with the customer in mind drives innovation faster than any other business strategy, regardless of the industry. One of the greatest attributes of a solution-driven culture organization is approaching every issue with the customer in mind and working within the best framework to create value for the customer. A customer-centric solution creates value that transcends beyond time, which would translate to making your clients happy and good revenue for your organization due to repeat business or partnership. Each time organization solves a customer problem or pain point, they have just created an asset for its balance sheet, which in turn creates an opportunity for expanded market share. The mind of a solution-driven organization possesses a certain culture within its vision or core value. Enabling an innovation culture from a customer perspective is a vital element to the sustainability of the organization due to the rapid nature of the market environment today. The hyperactive nature of the business environment needs a culture that will be self-adaptable across different industry verticals and respond appropriately to customer demands.

This is a familiar ground most technical forward thinking organization find themselves, which complicate their deliverable and account for most portion of the engineered technical debt. There is always the temptation to speed up your execution for product launch even when the firm lacks the fundamentals, which is a bad practice when using a software solution firm, for example. The speed of delivery of solutions spans different industry verticals, but most of the product translates to value. This happens to be one great question that resonates in the mind of innovative leaders and consumers of the products in diverse market verticals. The concept of understanding your market requirements gives you better visibility on the best strategy to adopt to enable a value, and that's where the innovation culture could be enabled to capture all endpoints of the value chain. Much of the time is spent at this phase, as the requirements will keep evolving to meet the needs of constructing the solution. The mapping of the solution is targeted toward creating each component and feature that solve the paint point.

Having a good grasp of this solution concept as a firm would give the project a better acceleration and elimination of backlog. Understanding your market gives you a broader picture of the best to enable the technology environment and calibrate it to suit the enterprise's growth journey. The market picture should help the organization gain good insight into the best strategy to construct a great foundational system that would respond to constant market change. The enterprise should be designed to embrace the future, which is always evolving because of some un-control entities, which is completely external, as an organization without such a setup will always react to the market, making it very difficult to execute change. Having a good understanding of your market space enables you to develop effective planning, factoring in all internal and external factors that could change the strategic equation of your organization.

Change is one skill set that was never taught in the traditional academia but is learned within the professional journey regardless of your industry. Organizational leaders should be change agents to drive the much-needed result and quickly react to any shift in direction to my good market demand. The concept of change is directly related to learning new ideas and being relevant to better processes, which is why firms that quickly adapt to new technology solutions create value for customers and shareholders. Countless products have made way to drain the budget of many organizations, even with good positioning from a customer vantage point. However, the viability of these products was short-lived due to the simple reason the product vision should be circled both from a tactical and strategic point of view. The ideation of a product comes with a great burden of conviction, which the organization or production owner need to drive in a convincing manner. The addiction should come from you personally understanding the value or pain point the product is solving and better interpreting it on different consumer market channels.

The stakes are mostly high in the construction of this value point because what drives the messenger here is the conviction and ability to curate the final deliverables. Organizations with leaders who are addicted to change spin the growth direction in an agile manner; through an open concept management style, which is more of a traditional daily walk around to check where issues exist among different teams and provide guidance for the team. Leaders should be adept at identifying constraints that will limit innovation and ideation within the organization's work stream based on a different scenario of solving the problem. To remain relevant to industry practices, all organizational leaders should be trained regularly with various tools that would help them execute their responsibilities in a very effective way.

Chapter Two

Stimulate Innovation Internally

We live in a world where most folks want an innovative product, but adapting to innovation millstones is a major issue, regardless of industry. It has become a natural burden for executives to break the norm and steer Candice's conversation around innovation concepts in the execution of daily tasks. The shift from conventional thought of creating an adaptable ecosystem helps change management leaders across the enterprise to produce predicted results. Starting out with someone at the executive level to be the gatekeeper will help grow and mature all the technical components that could easily enable the business drivers. It is the duty of the chief technology officer to act as an evangelist or executive catalyst to naturally stimulate innovation across the board by incorporating core elements into every day-to-day function. The technology stack procured would determine how you intend to scale and disrupt your market verticals. The marketplace is actually not a friendly place, as it is structured to respond to fierce competition between defenders and challengers.

Defender market leaders are an organization that has been in business with great market share but finding it difficult to innovate to expand more share. While the challenger market leader is the organization that innovates in a rapid manner and launches to market to disrupt the market space and expand to new market shares. Having a good understanding of your backend and frontend is very important to drive growth. Encourage your team to take risks, always be open to failure, learn from it, and devise a better route to solve the problem. The concept starts with a culture, which has to be steered by the leaders within the organization. To better alter the culture involves incorporating input from both the combination of top and bottom initiatives to minimize or eliminate resistance. Change is a journey and not a place, and organizational leaders need to understand that everyone in the organization is a change agent, meaning they are change agents that can enable the change philosophy. There are various factors to consider when planning stimulating innovation, and these factors create the atmosphere for the expected desired outcome.

Technology firms have noticed some rapid form of innovation drive across their organization through the adoption of open source community in software development, through direct target business value creation, as a result of community-based knowledge sharing platforms. The open development environment will naturally enablable participation by any individual or organization, including competing organizations which creates a great knowledge-sharing hub overall when your firm becomes a member or participant. One concept an innovative platform would stimulate is openness across the board, apart from encouraging merit-based participation principle, where newcomers are invited to participate based on their past proven merit and competency.

Develop a clear strategy

Define a clear strategy that everyone in the organization will take ownership of, as a better strategy should help clarify the expectation of all employees when it comes to problem-solving. Developing a good innovation strategy helps the employees with clarity about the core role of innovation and further reinforces the fact that innovation is everyone's responsibility. Defining a good innovation core principle in the mission framework enforces it on the organizational leadership to think about what innovation means to them and enable in clear terms how their employees should contribute new ideas for products, solutions, systems, and services.

No organization wants to waste resources, but it will serve a great value to accept failure and make it a norm to thrive in the current evolving world. Every organization that wants to disrupt must come to the reality that is always acknowledging the possibility of failure,de-dramatize it, and encouraging risky initiatives will always help employees approach innovation in a more open and inventive way. History has always shown that current market leaders like Amazon and Netflix have never shied away from acknowledging their past failures. An example of a firm that enables innovation at every value chain of their operational execution strategy is Microsoft, through the enablement of innovation component in their employee's day-to-day tasks. As Coca-Cola CEO James Quincey puts it, "If we're not making mistakes, we are not trying hard enough."

An excellent way of managing innovation strategy is to accept the reality factor of mistakes and work around them for great value creation. Your strategy should be fluid in nature to accommodate for any change in scope or direction as the business evolves to adapt to the competitive advantage in the market. Your strategy should be agile in nature, not just to accommodate for speed of execution, but flexibility through capturing the real-valued objectives to clients. A strategy is active when at any point in time, which could be adjusted to fit into the direction of the organization through core value creation in all the business domains of the organization.

A clear strategy is an enabler of great catalyst across organizations regardless of industry verticals; an example could be seen from firms that have evolved over the years to create value for customers with a constant change of regulations across the world, showing the power of having a clear strategy and re-engineering the strategy to meet up with changing times.

Identify innovative vendors as Partners

It is very important to identify solution providers that have specific niche services that are aligned with your ecosystem, which will result in identifying suitable technology partners. A good enterprise landscape should provide a piece of insider information on a technological solution that has the capabilities to simplify your business operations. Designing an internal tracker of vendor solutions that solve complex problems in business and make great industry connections will help perform comparative analysis at the early stage before any form of partnership can be established for both parties. It is advisable to consider utilizing best-of-breed tools for the foundation of your ecosystem of those innovative players with that you have developed unique relationships.

While the internet pool of searches in identifying technology partners is good, it will have some shortfall due to public or editor opinion and does not guarantee continued innovation afterwards. An understanding better picture of your future vision helps you envision your ecosystem with your technological landscape and align the framework to identify partners that is fit for the ecosystem. It is also very important for executives to spend a good time reviewing your industry ecosystem and flexible node points that are flexible to tie your business orientation with change management, future business models, and innovative technology partners.

Adopt Experimentation initiative

No firm can truly innovate without adopting an experimentation culture to explore opportunities. There must be an appetite to create something new either through customer co-creation, participation in an innovation hub, and identifying market adjacencies. The concept of adjacencies is new products or markets that are closely related to the work a company is currently executing in, but are different enough to represent new value for the organization. The bold move to these areas would make the organization creates new customers and solidifies its market position. The strategy of looking for market adjacencies is one core enabler in a forward-thinking organization that would always outlive its competitors. There is a great need to embrace co-creation and open innovation opportunities, which helps accelerate activities by involving your customers at any point in time to create value. Participation in an innovation hub is another channel to drive innovation, as it recognizes the importance of a multidisciplinary approach to innovation and stimulates collaboration in problem-solving, which ultimately translates to good "blue-sky" thinking at the enterprise level of the organization.

Every breakthrough technology goes through a thorough phase or lifecycle that starts with experimentation, firms should be ready to take this risk to be very competitive with the evolution of times. Some organization doesn't make a budget that will accommodate for this risk at an enterprise level, but it is the responsibility of the chief technology officer to own this initiative and drives it with compelling value before all major stakeholders in all tie of the organization. Data meant nothing to most firms twenty-five years ago, but due to the vast pool of data experimentation over the years, it has proven to help excellent business support systems, which range from an effective marketing campaign, management of consumer behavior, and good insight to a new market and strategy execution. Every team leads in an organization should be regularly trained in the art of idea experimentation to better lead as the change catalyst.

There is a great need for an organization to look beyond the traditional research and development unit to proffer ideas but should open up a research-driven environment among employees. Ideation from a diverse pool could easily create value across multiple value chains in the organization but should be stored at a centralized location and updated regularly to support effective decision support systems. An organization with a good approach to adapting to change and competing in the future needs to adopt a research-oriented strategy in its day-to-day task execution, which makes it very imperative for the organization to build this traction.

There are some factors that play out to stimulate innovation externally, as a result, being in an organization that has a traditional mindset to change. Then it is very important to consider trusted partners or vendors that would help your organization enable innovation externally, which is where your knowledge-sharing channel is open to driving the changing culture. Enabling innovation culture externally is very tough because of the resistance from both the lower and upper management in an organization, which some time due to reasons best known to them. Some of the issues range from job loss, learning difficulty, lack of ability to adapt, and lack of formal education. Lack of knowledge within the organization is another major reason why an external catalyst is needed to create that enablement in all layers of the organization, where knowledge sharing could help drive the needed change.

The strategy to enable change in an organization through external channels comes in a different flavor, which is that partnerships like outsourcing and direct-targeted training are great means of enabling external innovation in an organization. Data is at the core of driving any technological change in any organization, providing clear information about past and current operations and predicting the future based on external forces.

Integrated collaborate environment

True innovation starts with transparent communication across the enterprise, it is the duty of the organizational leaders to steer the vision as stewards of the value. Open communication among leaders and employees always helps drive innovation maturity at all layers of any organization, regardless of size. It helps employees execute their day-to-day task right with good speed due to the expanded information sharing among team members through the promotion of innovation and problem-solving techniques at the domain -the enterprise level. The workspace design and layout are other great catalysts for better open communication through team co-location for better collaboration and cross-information sharing among integrated teams for product or service initiatives. The need to execute observable transactions within an organization, in short, is needed now to meet the increasing capacity of the ever-changing business community and industry verticals, which require the robust deployment of transparent technology solutions across multiple nodes regardless of location and time zone.

The need to reach out to diverse stakeholders increases the complexities of technology operations, which require robust transactions that will support ever-demanding changing needs. Industry experts over the last decade have raised the issue of the speed of open transactions among vendor partners who are end users of these solutions and have recommended the application of technology which are data-driven. Despite realizing the impact cloud technology might have on their industry, companies seem hesitant to dedicate resources to explore and improve better optimization, which is a fair point, as security is a major factor to consider before adopting the technology solution. The global technology community is currently facing many complex interfaces with partners around the world, including robust collaboration tools. Industry experts within the technology community have been driving the value of diverse security technologies, which will enable speed of transactions and transparency in platforms.

Another key area organizational leaders should look at will be to establish a well-defined strategy for a multi-channel way of combating ideas and attitudes that destroy innovation through the promotion of communication that generates innovation. A good example of how to stimulate innovation in a team environment is to encourage contribution among all team members in any meeting. Such an act would create an open environment where all opinions and thoughts are expressed, which could translate to a viable solution to an existing problem.

Open communication could easily inspire passion among employees to deliver consistent value to the market. Today's workspace is in great demand for an intentional, collaborative enterprise environment of shared workload. In addition, should be secure and compliant collaboration solutions that could integrate multiple capabilities, including voice, video, messaging, chat and task management, enabling the context of conversations to persist across multi-platform channels and device agnostic. A great collaborative landscape could be greatly engineered to solve complex enterprise problems within a short time frame, as buying –from all subject matter experts and organizational sponsors could easily review and approve due to better information visibility.

A digital journey requires understanding your technical environment, and align stacks that are adaptable to rapid change for the future, and eliminating any barrier to future growth or expansion. The adoption of flexible technology solutions within your enterprise simplifies the decision-making process because of the real-time information flow that provides insightful analytics within the open digital environment. A great collaborative tool should be able to touch and impact every part of your business operations to better stimulate digital initiatives. As a leader, it is imperative to engage vendors that have a robust solution that would cut down all silo walls within your organization. Collaboration has become a way of life for innovation to thrive with the speed of technology evolution, it will help review the best-aligned solution in real-time among team members and eliminate redundancy overall within the enterprise based on the short adoption cycle. While there is a need for better collaborative tools across teams and enterprises, it is very imperative to bring tools that stimulate safe collaboration to track tasks.

Creating an integrated collaborative platform at the enterprise level has shown to create productivity, where multiple vendors could plug in different technology solutions and enable seamless integration with other in-house applications in the organization.

Organizational Behavior

The concept of innovation comes with risk, which they should not feel threatened as seen in the traditional organization today. Modern organizations are constantly reviewing their people policy and how it reflects on how to target a good talent pool and drive innovative ways to retain afterwards. Establishing the candor to ensure staff psychological safety is very important to stabilize the environment. Develop a good reward system to recognize and reward any successful innovations, as such initiatives would stimulate natural innovation among employees and enable the best out of employees, and could translate to new ideas for market disruption. The organizational policies should reflect a flexible approach to create a more diverse pool that would attract and retain the best talent.

The pre-pandemic era never showed us anything much about how to create a flexible working environment, like expanding the geographical location of the talent pool. There is a great need for business leaders to look inward to revolutionize the way their organizations pivot and shift by combining the intelligence of data with new emerging capabilities in a way that creates holistic, customized user experiences that help people perform at their best. Organizational engagement and productivity are tied to the scope of technology adoption at a different layer of the organization, and leaders should imagine a technology that could easily be customized to fit into the organizational mission to eliminate any downtime with any change in organizational strategy.

Developing and growing a shared strategy will create a robust enterprise that the leaders would be able to establish a credible technology solution budget that is aligned to the continuous improvement landscape. In addition, the buy-in of establishing a digital ecosystem starts with a design that captures the thoughts or input because it is a shared responsibility.

It is very imperative to have a better understanding of aligning your idea with a key performance indicator that could measure both the quick win and long-term strategic gain. Best-in-class continuous improvement techniques should have a definite partnership mechanism across all layers of the organization for better results. The post-pandemic has been able to accelerate the technology adoption journey because of the value of remaining competitive in the marketplace, which is a great shift from the pre-pandemic organizational culture. Technology solutions have helped to shape the organizational culture of most businesses and will require the re-skill of the entire workforce to deliver targeted value for shareholders.

Embrace Open Source

The emergent technology future heavily relies on the open source community to enable seamless innovation across different organizations. The appetite to establish great quality systems for your software applications makes open source projects valuable to stimulate innovation across your business enterprise environment. Solution development firms over the years have been able to establish a compelling reason why open source is best to drive innovation and reduce the cost of business applications. Some of the benefits are;

a. Zero vendor dependence: the open source eliminate any form of locked-in relationship with a vendor regarding a particular software company. With the existence of the code in the open space, it becomes possible to evolve your business solutions based on your desired support without constraint.
b. Good code quality: The involvement of lost developers adding code refinement in the open source helps produce code with fewer flaws compared to the standard commercial developed application.
c. Improved security: The value of having many developers working on source code means identifying security problems at a good speed. The large pool of developers within the project will help multiple resources to fix bugs or upgrade the code without relying on a proprietary vendor.

d. Better control and license management: The open source provides an opportunity for developers to have better control on how to use the code because a proprietary application is fully controlled by the developers. Unlike the commercial license, an organization could use the application or software as many times as possible with little or no restrictions.

Chapter Three

Resolving the Complexity in Your Organizational Landscape

The rise in technology complexities in business processes needs an enterprise architecture framework that is focused on organizational goals. Good planning is needed at this phase, as building and deploying systems is not a goal. Designing responsible models of the organization and systems are key to establishing a comprehensive primary goal that will help eliminate duplicative systems and enable targeted business-centric strategic goal. The CIO should drive the value of adopting a disciplined approach of making sure the enterprise architecture focuses on systems behavior and interaction to achieve organizational goals.

The aspect of engagement across the organization provides a better view of how best to respond-to-respond to changes and policies will help enable core functional capabilities within the organization. The maturity of the organization platform could easily be captured by the enterprise architect based on the value of information of overserving and understanding the emergent behaviors of the systems. The evolution of technologies has gradually changed the optics of how solutions could be deployed to organizations to support their operations seamlessly. The effort from enterprise architects at every organization helps translates operational tools that business leaders could utilize to steer the direction of the organization.

Finally, developing a performance measurement will be helpful to effectively respond on going changes in the enterprise behaviors, and incrementally progress towards the desired goals. It is very important to note that you cannot eliminate complexities in organizations, but you can structure the fundamentals process orientation to simplify the enterprise while modernizing your operational landscape with growing business requirements.

Consolidate Your Data for Innovation

Establish a clear picture of where your data resides, design a well-defined strategy of how you want to place your data for the future through the elimination of barriers, and incorporate all regulatory data privacy best practices. The current data privacy landscape is yet to gain maturity status, due to a lack of standardization across the board, most especially in North America, thus making it very difficult for the business to innovate. Europe currently has the most matured data privacy regulation that safeguards the customers, but it comes with a heavy price.

The process of consolidating your Data gives a better approach to aligning your business operation with all existing regulations. The regulation has kind of put a limit on how much customer data you can exploit to maximize better revenue. The aggregation of your business operational data gives a better view to plan both short-term and strategic scope in mind. Data itself means nothing if normalized to support effective decision-making processes from all business and transactional interfaces.

The consolidation of your data should reflect the long-term strategic direction of the organization to embrace the future to evolve with changing demands to customer's needs. There is some flavor of governance needed to establish a sound foundational design structure, so some factors to consider are very important at this phase of the data modernization journey. It is very important to keep an open mind when reviewing all the considerations for the future and try to design a decoupled foundation that will be very flexible to consolidate for the future. The gathering of the vital components of the data strategy is needed here to develop a comprehensive enterprise view and to enable executives to design a long-term roadmap that can be measured. A good data platform should have a define interface with other platforms and enable agnostic characteristics to adopt any form of data synchronization as the organization expands operations to new markets regardless of geographical location.

Great data fundamentals should be defined in consistent business rules that factor a diverse pool of business operations will would require the designer to utilize complex use case which is tailored to various business orientation. The presence of complexities in the technology ecosystem in the organization will enhance the risk that could trigger problems within the various platforms in the market space because of a lack of observability. The integration of technology solutions within the digital transaction framework was meant to resolve the unidentified problem of observability of information within the system because increased business operations management has some complexities within functional requirements, particularly if the platform engages multiple data consumptions.

The consolidation of your data should capture all information that gives the business entity the relationship overview at the basic model level. Good consolidation of your organization's data creates a dynamic scheme for the enterprise to optimize your data for effective use across the different domains in the organization. Optimization of the enterprise data would enable an efficient platform, which can take on multiple meanings to diverse stakeholders and overall saves 80 per cent of productivity time in publishing customizable report systems. What organizations do with enterprise available Data is countless in today's dynamic market evolution, which takes a forward-thinking approach to harness the power of that opportunities. There are many benefits to consolidating your organizational data in one enterprise pool, which are;

- Merger and acquisition
- Privacy regulation
- Customization
- Better workflow
- Operation insight
- Modernization roadmap
- Optimization
- Automation

Merger and Acquisition

The major issue arising from lots of mergers and acquisitions of the organization is harmonization of data, which could delay the completion of the merger from months to over a year. The lack of consolidation of Data is very critical to modernizing the organization's technology landscape, which establishes the criticality of these components to design a good strategy for the overall environment. It is advisable for organizational leaders to set up a good agnostic platform that would be able to connect to other technology solutions for seamless migration.

That is the reason why it is critical to select a technology stack that is easy to upgrade, cheap to maintain, and integrates. Harmonization of your business fundamentals will help identify all assumptions when dealing with stakeholders among merging parties to better establish the Meta data that is needed to define a perfect synergy to stimulate innovation regardless of geography of operation.

Privacy Regulation

The setup of different data set is based on responding to the functional orientation of the business landscape because of the privacy act in the region of operation. The foundational data structure is critical to the growth direction of the firm, which mostly starts with a defined strategy of aggregating all the data structure based on their core business value and aligning the business strategy to properly accommodate future growth. The nature of privacy law is very complex due to variations in different regions of the world. It is in the place of best industry practice to establish a fragmented-decouple data structure that will take into consideration different legislation globally, which could be updated regularly with defined governance.

There is a grey line between best business practice and conducting regular private impact assessment to review your risk threshold, thus making privacy a vital core element, especially in customer data-driven organizations. Organizations that have matured privacy within their business operations have the tendency to scale faster to meet customer needs.

Customization

The organization that utilizes universal configuration at a foundational level is bound not to face an un-predicted obstacle when planning to adopt scalabilities across the business domain. The level of data customization is a pointer to the direction of the organization from both strategic and tactical perspectives. Having a good understanding of your data landscape will help identify your workaround in designing your configuration management. The core data that are fundamental to your organization's operation will help drive the customization initiative to fits into a list of multiple options because of meeting customers' needs. The configuration of the right type of technology in an enterprise landscape organization stimulates efficiencies as all the known departmental deliverables must be well defined, which could translate to an optimized value chain across your business line.

Customizations create flexibility along the innovation pipeline, thereby altering structured processes within your business enterprise platform. The change that comes with customizing your business data provides perspective in handling day-to-day. Most current platforms have now automated their configuration to any form of the desired customization, which makes it easier to develop a workable strategy from the start of your plans.

Adopt Containerization

The organization needs to package all critical applications, which helps them scale efficiently apart from minimizing the impact of attack of the business application due to breach. The advantages that come with packaging your applications are enormous, which are; easier management, improved security, agility, portability, availability, and flexibility. The technology and business leadership in brownfield organization that has lots of existing application should greatly consider migrating all their application that is critical to their business operation to the container environment. It is much easier for the green field environment due to the availability of information from the front end, as the organizational setup is still in the setup or planning phase.

Develop Your Cloud Strategy

Designing a classic cloud strategy should start with reflecting on your organization's technology budget. There should be a comprehensive review of the business strategy, which will involve capturing inventories of all your critical applications and performing fundamental analysis of on-prem vs cloud. The cloud strategy will identify the transition action plan the organization will take to implement the application in the new cloud environment. The underlying environment is among the critical component to consider. Are there dependencies within the cloud environment that will require optimizing the application before migration? Do we just lift and shift to the new environment? What is the cost model of the intended cloud environment? How best can we optimize resource utilization for better computing?

All the above considerations could easily be resolved through the development of a robust strategy with the following business-use case tied to the overall strategy of the organization.

a. Cost management
b. Establish a compelling goal of moving to the cloud

c. Data regulation and policies
d. Security

Modernization Roadmap

A technology roadmap is a strategic enablement direction that lists the current state of your technology assets and your future desired state and identify what it takes to get to the future state. The gap process will unravel the needed project that will modernize the technology platform, which will be classified based on the priority and budget valuation of the organization. The roadmap will detail all the level information by activities that need to be done to get to the future state. Developing detailed plans with comprehensive information on your current assets will provide a better understanding of both your cost centre, and identify the best approach to reduce the cost to create a tangible deliverable for business. The roadmap should be able to clearly identify the enterprise risk based on proposed solution options in the modernization strategy and classify the risk versus reward driver for the executives to review.

The days of the traditional business landscape are over, and the current business environment is pressured to innovate to remain competitive. A classic technology platform is needed to enable some core capabilities of an organization, which brings in the concept of the plug-in to your business orientation with a good technology ecosystem. Business executives should tie the big picture concept before adopting any form of technology stacks. The harmonization of different technology systems expands the complexities of the business process in the organization, and designing an adaptable ecosystem will overall help with the best value for money in your technology spend. It is very vital to look out for the technology ecosystem and platforms within your industry verticals and review in detail players that might come in to disrupt your business model. The research will help in classifying all the available platforms in the market and align them with a good ecosystem to enable value creation. Democratization of your resources will increase productivity within the various business functional domain in your organization, which will help establish a strategic model that would move the organization from a reactive to a proactive stance. A very important factor to consider before democratizing your organization's resources would be to establish a guiderails to control all internal policies effectively.

Establish an ecosystem that involves customer experience to create industry cross thinking, as digital transformation is currently the catalyst to our traditional business ecosystems, which are fast fading away in traditional markets. It is very imperative for organizations to have a 360 view of the entire ecosystem based on a different business use case to enable tangle value. It is imperative for organizational leaders to clearly understand the difference between context architecture and designing a technology strategy that is 100 per cent tied to enterprise strategy. It will start with making technology strategy a subset of the organizational business strategy, thus making it easy to be flexible to changing business requirements. The candid advice to leaders is to develop a best-in-class communication procedure that is all-inclusive to drive agility across the enterprise, which event could be measured at any point in time.

It will be great if organizations develop classic metrics for evaluating technology investment, where the return on investment could be captured and tracked based on the implementation maturity within the business community of the organization. And doing so will create a good mechanism in place that will foster intra-ecosystem innovation beyond the current traditional research and development model. Such a strategy will easily galvanize ideas from other external organizations, including partners.

The direct pressure on the global business community is altering the slow walk of programs to enable quick wins in the digital transformation journey through direct-targeted collaboration between innovation partners. Establishing such partnerships will stimulate the desired agile environment that is aligned with other digital ecosystem partners. Any system you do not measure, you cannot improve. Therefore, it will be very important to establish metrics to measure your complete ecosystem and track the improvement of your innovation block that is supporting your business landscape.

Business leaders should have a clear perspective on how the internal technology platform is creating targeted value across the organization's enterprise environment and the entire various business domain. Having that basic knowledge as a business leader helps you invest in technologies that will create multi-layered value for the organization. The establishment of good metrics will help organizational leaders identify a program that would enable value-driven modernization of technology from both a strategic and tactical standpoint. It is advisable for organization leaders to utilize the technology adoption cycle to establish better control of enterprise risk in the multi-layer domain of the organization. Having a great idea or the desire to adopt a good technology solution to drive the business environment requires a thorough review of identifying your requirements and how best to map the solution to meet the desired need. The adoption cycle could be customised to fit in alignment with the enterprise business goals of the organization.`

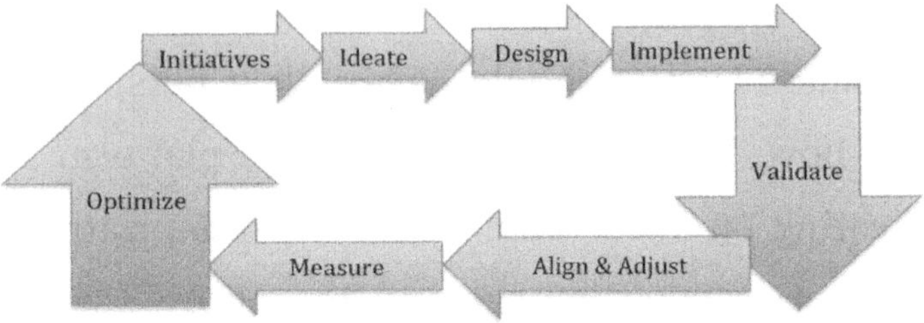

Technology solution adoption cycle Fig A

Initiatives: Every great solution starts with initiatives that should solve the business problem to enable value for the organization. It could be enabled by anyone in the organization but managed in a disciplined manner to gain a quick win for the sponsor.

Ideate: The program initiative will translate to the idea that needs to be modified to make it more viable. This phase capture all the requirement to better construct the solutions that will solve the business problem. It will involve designing a classic requirement matrix that should be able to resolve any solution issue.

Design: The solution is designed at this phase based on the output of the requirement from different business domains and the overall enterprise. The design concept should reflect on future growth direction by enabling a complex technology environment with minimal effort while modernizing the ecosystem.

Implement: The solution implemented at this phase based on the original design concept will help manage the core-desired deliverables.

Validate: The solution is validated with the intended targeted value, which involves checking with requirements and the designed solution.

Align & Adjust: The solution is aligned and adjusted to fit into the technology ecosystem. This is iterative in nature to achieve targeted value.

Measure: The solution is measured and tracked with better plug-ins with the business communities because it becomes very imperative to note where the current solution gap exists. As it is often said, "Anything you can't measure, you can't improve," establish the reason to always design a system that is measurable to plan for future improvement.

Optimize- this phase centered on the maturity of the technology solution before working on leveraging and optimizing for better and greater value creation

Design your data to respond to different market region Regulations.

There is a need to review your data landscape and define a classic pathway on how best to design a system that would effectively respond to customers regardless of location. The rise in different data laws and regulations is giving the business community some ambitious view to design a harmonized data interface that can easily invoke different regional government data policies in real-time in a simplified manner.

Establishing foundational data systems that will handle customer information in a responsible manner within the market of operation is key to remaining competitive. Understanding your market region will better prepare the business enterprise to configure there day to day operations to the needs of the business driven by robust technology solutions. The business leaders of the organization should consider their future expansion phase and establish an operating environment that could easily adopt quick plug-in within multi-regional operations that supports global clients. Designing a flexible model that could harmonize heterogeneous regulations is key to quickly adapting a good change management process, as rigid technology platforms will greatly limit the business opportunities of organizations expanding to new markets. The organizational leaders should make sure the enterprise architect adopt a modernization roadmap that establishes how to handle customer information in the different market region in the future.

Establish Enterprise Governance for Innovation

There is a school of thought that says" governance limits innovation" and is not true, as you are simply putting control in place to manage the overall environment. You cannot manage what you cannot control, which means developing good control is the first place to start and design a measurable key performance indicator. Clear governance should be able to orchestrate change, not be a constraint to creativity, as it just requires a process mechanism that is shared cross-enterprise collaboration.

The design and implementation of good governance would establish better control of your enterprise environment, thereby giving you a great ability to manage the gradual growth of your organization. There are various factors to consider here when it comes to data management. You would need to define a good guardrail to manage good enterprise workflow operation, as good governance would act as a system mechanism that controls all entities, processes, resources, and people to align with business goals. There is always a thin line between tight and flexible governance, a tight governance limit innovation and makes it very difficult to evolve over time, thus making it difficult to rapidly respond to the market with new product and creating a static atmosphere. Flexible governance can rapidly respond to innovation within a short time frame, for example, when an organization is expanding from North America to Europe, the pricy act of customer information is critical here because of the tight privacy regulation that exists in that region. This makes it very difficult to operate in the different regions without retooling the organization governance framework that suits that region due to different privacy acts-regulations in that country. A good flexible governance framework should be able to stimulate innovation across the board regardless of the region of operation of the firm. The essence of governance to innovation is to have some form of control mechanism in place to manage ethics, risk, compliance, and other administration elements in a way that would adapt to changing times of different market verticals.

The concept of data governance will clearly drive the speed of innovation, as some of the models will slow or speed up the enterprise enablement. The design of your measurement scope will give you a good baseline for continuous management improvement. There are core metrics needed to evaluate the innovation journey, either from a domain perspective or enterprise level, and establish a robust key performance indicator used to track the improvement. There is a great need to also critically look at the speed of execution, which is a vital element to enable scalability in operations across all business units. The subject of achieving complete transactions between a client organization and partners requires good system integration from both ends while adopting an enterprise platform visible enough that can respond well to the business strategy.

The consolidation of the enterprise platform is very important to manage the overall ecosystem; as such, the direction will pivot the environment enablement across different business functions. It is very imperative to review the fundamentals of your organization and align all processes with the organizational visions before optimizing the technology platform. The governance framework should be deployed to enable a program that will capture a great value that is tied to specific business goals for the organization. Great governance will naturally stimulate innovation across the enterprise regardless of the location.

Automate Your Landscape

Review your complete business process orientation, and calibrate the right technology stacks that fit into the overall business operations. The target value to create at this phase is to automate all repeatable tasks to improve the efficiency of your operational value chain. It all starts with the definition of the organization's standard operating procedure (SOP), which is very foundational from the planning phase. The planning phase will provide the opportunity for organizational leaders to design a procedure that could easily be adjusted to better align to good measurement metrics both at a strategic and tactical level. The best approach is to start with designing your organizational process orientation based on best industry practices within your industry verticals, which is comprehensive in nature due to extended detail information modeling at both the front and back end.

Identify all the repeated tasks within various business domains, followed by reviewing the level of effort required to complete a task and map every layer of error that could occur based on the human-machine interaction interface. The next step will be to classify the error threshold and designate a scoring pattern, and there is a great need to review your overall information architecture landscape to resolve any hidden constrain across all business operational interfaces. The cases are different for both brown field and green field organizations, especially if you are implementing automation in large corporations. Industry research has proven that automation can also be implemented in any organization regardless of size. There will be little effort to implement in new organizations compared to an older organization that has an existing legacy structure. Conclusively, make sure your planning phase should reflect on the evolution of your industry to design a more robust and agile organization.

Chapter Four

Cluster Your Framework with Compelling Governance

The idea of understanding your landscape will provide a better way or approach to harness great value from enterprise governance, which is based on the following core- data management areas.

- Data Architecture
- Data Modeling and design
- Data storage and operations
- Data security
- Data integration and interoperability
- Documents and content
- Reference and master data
- Data warehousing and business intelligence (BI)
- Metadata
- Data quality

Data Policy

Data policy is a policy that contains overall data management policies, which include a defined set of rules, stated principles, and comprehensive frameworks of the enterprise. The overall purpose of the policy is meant to provide guidelines both at the detail and strategic level across the different areas of the data organizations. Data policy, which in most cases is not given great attention, has made it very difficult to exploit many initiatives by compromising customers' information, and this comes with a hefty price to resolve. The acquisition and onboarding of new customers come with an increase in the data information of your organization. In addition, this information span different geographical location, which requires a different setup based on data regulation. Data policy is segmented into a multi-layered framework that captures the business enterprise operational model. They are a set of rules that govern the overall compliance plans of the organization. A bad data policy in an organization will not just be a constraint but also compromise the overall security data architecture of the business enterprise.

Data policy definition should be clear enough to accommodate the expansion or growth of the organization in both the short and long term. The core journey of a great data policy in organizations starts with a classic business case to establish a robust policy that could be reviewed regularly to capture any changing regulations. The vital element to start with in constructing a good data policy is defining clear metrics to improve the process in an ongoing manner. The involvement of diverse stakeholders will ensure the policy is granular enough to capture all known and unknown issues from the front end before the document becomes a living policy in organizations.

The rise in different regulations around the world should make business executives design agile policies that reflect updated review quarterly to better safe guide customers' information. You must have noticed a rise in multiple law suite across different regions of the world because of different regulations by different government agencies across the world. Designing a robust data framework will leverage people, processes, and technologies with compliance for data access with the organization's business orientation. The framework should hold best practice elements of your organization's privacy policy, which includes a classic definition of identity, access management, and consent management. The policy definition should address all the risk factors currently faced by organizations today. There is a need to establish a well-defined process listed below to be able to mitigate the privacy risk with your business regardless of the region of operation.

1. Establish cross-functional data ownership and awareness for better knowledge sharing
2. Streamline data policies and procedures to capture changing regulations based on the best practice framework
3. Consider upgrading technology and infrastructure to respond to customers or regulatory authorities
4. Create an adaptable model to respond to new regulations and reputational management, and enable enterprise-wide transparency

Monetize Your Data and Gain a Competitive Advantage

The rapid change of business –the operational landscape is constantly affecting the maturity cycle of technology overall, regardless of the industry vertical. In addition, it has caused a shift from the traditional business norm to creating a strategy that is fluid in nature, which has created lots of flexibility that organization could customize their intended solution. Monetization of data can only be executed in a matured data enterprise that has a democratized framework while invoking diverse data policies at the same time. It is vital to review the business framework of your day-to-day operations and capture the node point of all valuable data that would be segmented for deep-dive analytics. Understanding your Data is very important in the journey of monetizing your landscape. Innovation culture is a continuous task which requires everyone in the organization to be naturally stimulated to strive to support change in a productive way, which means organizations that have innovative cultures are naturally in a dynamic state. It takes a great collaborative effort from all business domains within the organization to deliver value from their units that could be targeted towards monetization strategy. An example of steering innovation culture could be pulled from Bezos's popular saying, "If you stop acting like a start-up, you are no longer innovating". The concept of "Day one "in amazon is built around innovation, which should be consistent at all times.

The organization that has a better handle on good data management can easily predict good market dominance, as they can unlock great capabilities from the multi-layers value chain of the business enterprise. The growth of the data stream within an organization to support day-to-day operations requires a great conceptual meta-data foundation to respond effectively to rapid organizational change. This is where some great advantage comes in handy regarding utilizing better valuation from data that can be monetised across different verticals. The change in the business landscape always creates the need for organizations to adapt at a rapid speed and creates an opportunity to monetize data. The journey to data monetization needs gradual improvements in people, processes, and technology to harness the value. The evolution of agile data-driven organization has changed the concept of how best to identify business capabilities within an enterprise ecosystem and help plan a well-planned targeted strategy that will enable a responsive platform.

Designing a good meta-data that captures your harmonized enterprise environment helps visualize a schema that could be very useful in the monetization journey. Therefore, identifying your toolbox is essential to enable an agile environment to scale better before any form of data democratization. The adoption of some outsource hosted platforms can help.

Chapter Five

Conclusion

Developing a flawless relationship between various business domain and the technology units to align and deliver targeted values both for short and strategic period require reflective planning at an enterprise level. The deployment of the framework should be designed in a disciplined manner through the embedment of technology solutions across functional boundaries of the organization, thereby democratizing data from multiple business domains and creating a sustainability innovation journey. The leadership in the organization should reflect on a major strategic plan that could enable easy technology plug-in across the enterprise, which will allow effective operations, regardless of the size of the expansion. Organizational leaders should reflect on the complete value chain intending to create within each business domain across the enterprise to better establish the needed transformational program. There is a candid need to review the current ecosystem by right-sizing the human interface with process and technology to deliver stellar results that could easily be measured and improved upon at every milestone of the organization.

It is very imperative for organizational leaders to understand how digital transformation works, to grow the information awareness of the risk of the enterprise environment, and overall will help translate security risk into people-oriented philosophy. Thus, it will help the organization create a measurable strategy that could be tracked and adjusted at every point in time to reflect the health check direction of the business. Create a data model that will allow you to expand for the future, review your market landscape, and research the evolution of the industry where your organization operates to deliver a forward-thinking solution that could be able to meet the market of the future. There are certain attributes that characterize the market of the future, which are rapid change management, ease of adoption or plug-in, and simplification. There is a great need to design a system that is easy to maintain and reuse through the combination of multiple business domains within the business architecture to utilize a single application that requires little enhancement, which will seamlessly operate on the common data model. Design multi-regional data privacy to enable classic information consumption without compromising any legal risk because of the different data privacy regulations across different nations in the world. Establishing global market heterogeneous data privacy policies within your data systems will help to operate in a lean and efficient manner due to the ease of plug-in of technology to drive business operation during the expansion phase of the organization.

Design a comprehensive technology–business governance system, and establish a simple mechanism to manage the entire ecosystem. This phase establishes the strategic planning model that develops the overall road map that will introduce and retire any technology solution that will enable the business platform. A quarterly review of this roadmap by the organization leaders and enterprise architect will help the business environment pursue a disciplined approach in their modernization journey that will help them remain competitive in the marketplace. The total cost of ownership of technology is also reviewed at this phase while performing value engineering on all tooling components that will help drive a robust business operation. The era of different organizational divisions operating in the silo is over simply because they can create value, which has resulted in creating lots of bureaucracy that are toxic to the modern firm due to a lack of transparency and collaboration at the enterprise level. The modern business environment is enabled by highly intensive collaborative tools, which should be adopted early enough to help organizational leaders foster knowledge synergies. The choice of collaborative tool should be able to provide great operational visibility across the enterprise to effectively manage and control all internal and external entities of the organization. The rise in complexities of technologies and software applications that support business operations also raises the stakes for an organization to design a robust cyber-security program that would include comprehensive planning with preventive strategy, incident response, business impact analysis, disaster recovery, and business continuity.

The journey of establishing a responsive technology platform that is aligned to your business ecosystem is an all-inclusive program, which would require setting up educational systems in place to transfer the learning component to every employee and consultant in the organization in an efficient manner. A classic journey of a forward-thinking organization starts with embedding your people, process, and technology to drive your operations and enabling targeted value for the customers, including all layers of product /service stakeholders. The process becomes easy if the component of the existing technology platform is agnostic in nature and could seamlessly plug into future upgrades of other related technology solutions. Another aspect that should be carefully reviewed by the organizational leaders is the knowledge transfer of technology solutions within various business domains to operate firms that can be relevant for the future.

Reference

https://opensource.google/projects

https://www.managebt.org/book/introduction/introduction-to-business-technology/

https://www.inc.com/debbie-madden/jeff-bezos-says-you-should-treat-every-day-at-your-company-like-day-1-heres-why-hes-wrong.html

Made in the USA
Monee, IL
04 November 2026

67385330R00046